How Many Greats?

by Jacqui Briggs
illustrated by Maurice Manning

Chapter 1
Moving

"How do you like your new home, Zak?" Dad called, handing Mom a cardboard box labeled *kitchen*.

"It's cool!" said Zak. "And someone left us some soup." Zak read the note taped to a large pot. "Who is Aunt Helen?" he asked.

"Aunt Helen is my grandmother's sister," said Dad. He pointed to a house across the street where a friendly-looking older woman sat on the front porch. She waved and smiled at Zak.

Zak waved hello as Dad grabbed another box and said, "Let's keep unloading the truck. Aunt Helen will understand how busy moving day is. We'll visit with her later."

In a few days, the house was settled, and Mom invited Aunt Helen over for dinner. Aunt Helen seemed very happy to have Zak's family right across the street. Zak liked the older lady, but he was a little uncomfortable around her. He didn't know what to talk to her about.

Zak spent the summer playing outside and making new friends. He played baseball, biked, did cannonballs at the pool, and went fishing and hiking with his parents. Meanwhile, Aunt Helen spent a lot of time on her porch. Zak waved to her a lot, but he didn't talk to her often. She didn't seem to have many visitors.

Chapter 2
Zak Volunteers

Soon after school started, Mom and Zak visited Aunt Helen. "We're lucky to live so close to you," Mom said. "Zak would like to get to know you better. He's a great kid, and he really handles responsibility well."

"I'm sure of it," said Aunt Helen, grinning.

Mom smiled. "Zak and I talked, and we've determined something. Zak wants to volunteer to help you around the house."

"Is that right, Zak?" asked Aunt Helen.

"Yes, ma'am," Zak agreed nervously. He suddenly felt shy. "I can do yard work, take out the trash, or do anything else you need."

"Just let us know when you need anything," Mom said. "The school bus drops Zak off right in front of your house. He could even stop by on weekends, if you like. Just be sure one of you calls me to say where he is."

Aunt Helen smiled brightly. "Thank you. I would love some help around the house, Zak."

One warm October day, Aunt Helen needed some help raking leaves. She asked Zak to stop by. Zak got to work right after he got off the school bus. Sweat dripped down his nose, but he kept working. He would keep his promise! He tied the last bag closed as Aunt Helen came out onto the porch.

"Are you about ready for a cool drink, Zak?" Aunt Helen called cheerily. "I've got one ready for you. It's so sunny out today."

"Yes, I'm thirsty!" Zak replied as he wiped sweat off his forehead. "I'll just take this bag of leaves to the curb and then I'll come in."

Aunt Helen and Zak talked while he drank his juice. "Your daddy used to visit me all the time when he was your age," said Aunt Helen.

"At this house?" asked Zak. Aunt Helen nodded, and Zak tried to picture his dad as a kid. He had all sorts of questions for Aunt Helen, and she answered each one. It turned out that Zak was a lot like his dad.

Aunt Helen had a lot of funny stories. "One morning, your dad made breakfast for the two of us. We had potato chips and pudding for breakfast," she chuckled. "It was delicious."

That winter, Zak got off the school bus one day and saw that Aunt Helen's sidewalk was icy and her newspaper was still in her yard. He knew walking on ice was a safety issue for Aunt Helen, so he picked up her newspaper.

Unlike Aunt Helen, Zak loved to slide on the ice. With the newspaper in one hand, he slid and shouted, "The champion!" He waved the newspaper at his invisible fans.

That afternoon, Zak joined Aunt Helen at the piano. She asked him what he wanted to sing, and he cast his vote for songs from the time when Aunt Helen was a little girl.

"She'll be coming round the mountain when she comes!" they sang.

Chapter 3
Great Times

By the time spring came, Zak was stopping by Aunt Helen's house every day after school. Sometimes he helped with chores, but other times they just talked. One Friday in April, Zak raced up the steps to hand Aunt Helen her mail. He was in an especially good mood.

"How was school today?" Aunt Helen asked.

"It was really fun," Zak said. "In social studies, we learned about family trees. My teacher told us all about his family tree."

"How neat," Aunt Helen said. "Have you seen our family tree, Zak?" Zak shook his head. Aunt Helen thought for a moment, then said, "I'm not sure where it is, but you have a right to see it. Should we make a new one?"

"Yes!" Zak reached into his backpack for a pencil and paper.

"Well, you're at the bottom of the tree. Above you is your daddy, and above him is his mother—your Grandma Mary. Above her is Great-Grandma Grace," explained Aunt Helen. "I'd be beside your Great-Grandma Grace."

14

"That makes me your great-great aunt," Aunt Helen said, smiling as she helped Zak fill in his tree. "That sure is a lot of *greats.*"

"No, Auntie, you are my great-great-great-greatest aunt!" cried Zak, hugging her tight.

Respond to Reading

Summarize

Use details to help you summarize *How Many Greats?*

Character	Clue	Point of View

Text Evidence

1. How do you know *How Many Greats?* is realistic fiction? GENRE

2. How does Zak feel about Aunt Helen at first? POINT OF VIEW

3. Use what you know about suffixes to figure out the meaning of the word *cheerily* on page 9. SUFFIXES

4. Write about how Zak feels about helping his Aunt Helen. Give details that show his point of view. WRITE ABOUT READING

Compare Texts
Read about how people walk to help others.

Freedom Walk

Colton Lockner was just four years old on September 11, 2001. When he was nine, he heard about the America Supports You Freedom Walks. These walks are held to remember those lost in the 9/11 attacks and to honor America's troops.

Freedom Walk Facts

People have organized Freedom Walks in many states, including California, Michigan, and Virginia. They even take place overseas. Children of American soldiers sometimes attend school in other countries. Some of these schools organize Freedom Walks.

When Colton first read about the walks, his uncle was stationed in Iraq. Colton felt strongly about supporting the United States's troops as well as victims of 9/ll.

Colton wanted to have a Freedom Walk at school. He talked to the principal, who agreed that it was a great idea.

In 2005, Americans marched in Washington, D.C. to honor America's troops and the victims of 9/11.

Before long, others heard about the walk, and it became a community project. Colton expected about 75 walkers in his hometown of Sebring, Ohio, but 2,000 people turned out to walk! Colton still leads walks in Ohio today.

Make Connections

How do Colton's actions show that he is a good citizen? ESSENTIAL QUESTION

How are Zak and Colton similar? TEXT TO TEXT

Focus on Social Studies

What to Do

Step 1 ▶ Think of jobs in which someone helps others. Choose a family member or school worker who does that job and interview him or her.

Step 2 ▶ Ask questions such as these:

1. How do you help others in your job?

2. What kind of training do you need for your job?

3. Can you tell me about a time when you helped someone?

Step 3 ▶ Report what you learned to the class. Discuss whether you would be interested in doing this job and why.

Thinkmark

Setting

Where does *How Many Greats?* take place? When does it take place?

Characters

How would you describe Zak?

How would you describe Aunt Helen?

Sequence of Events

What happens at the **beginning, middle,** and **end** of *How Many Greats?*

Make Connections

What connections can you make between *How Many Greats?* and your own life?

Being a Good Citizen

GR P • Benchmark 38 • Lexile 620

Grade 2 • Unit 5 Week 1

www.mheonline.com

The *McGraw·Hill* Companies

ISBN-13 978-0-02-118973-1
MHID 0-02-118973-0

99701

EAN

9 780021 189731

2

Mc
Graw
Hill
Education

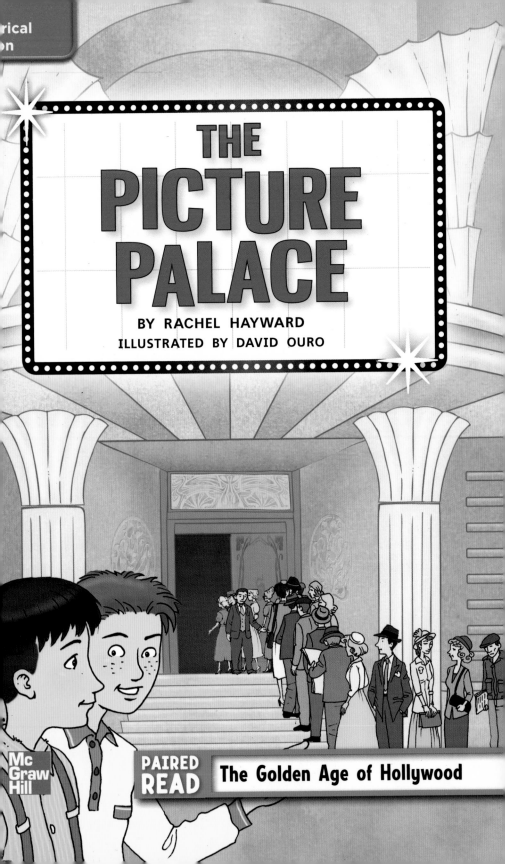

STRATEGIES & SKILLS

Comprehension

Strategy: Make Predictions
Skill: Compare and Contrast

Vocabulary Strategy

Idioms

Vocabulary

assume, guarantee, nominate, obviously, rely, supportive, sympathy, weakling

Content Standards

Social Studies
History

Word Count: 2,039**

**The total word count is based on words in the running text and headings only. Numerals and words in captions, labels, diagrams, charts, and sidebars are not included.

PROPERTY OF
**Cedar Rapids Community
School District**

Education

Send all inquiries to:
McGraw-Hill Education
Two Penn Plaza
New York, New York 10121

ISBN: 978-0-02-119196-3
MHID: 0-02-119196-4

Printed in China.

7 8 9 DSS 16 15

D